Homework Helpers
Maths

Ages 6–7
Key Stage 1/Year 2

Brian Speed & Linda Terry

 We're the Homework Helpers!

 We've thought up lots of fun activities for you!

 So grab your pens and pencils...

 ...and let's get started!

Longman

An imprint of **Pearson Education**

Harlow, England · London · New York · Reading, Massachusetts · San Francisco
Toronto · Don Mills, Ontario · Sydney · Tokyo · Singapore · Hong Kong · Seoul
Taipei · Cape Town · Madrid · Mexico City · Amsterdam · Munich · Paris · Milan

Series editors:
Stuart Wall & Geoff Black
*With thanks to Fay Turner for additional material and
Heather Ancient for editorial development work*

These people helped us write the book!

A complete range of **Homework Helpers** is available.

		ENGLISH	MATHS	SCIENCE
Key Stage 1	Ages 5–6 Year 1	✓	✓	Science is not included in the National Tests at Key Stage 1
	Ages 6–7 Year 2	✓	✓	
Key Stage 2	Ages 7–8 Year 3	✓	✓	✓
	Ages 8–9 Year 4	✓	✓	✓
	Ages 9–10 Year 5	✓	✓	✓
	Ages 10–11 Year 6	✓	✓	✓

This tells you about all our other books.

Which ones have you got?

Pearson Education Limited
Edinburgh Gate, Harlow
Essex CM20 2JE, England
and Associated Companies throughout the world

© Pearson Education Limited 2000

The right of Brian Speed and Linda Terry to be identified as authors of this work has been asserted in accordance with the Copyright, Designs and Patents Act 1988

All rights reserved; no part of this publication may be reproduced, stored in any retrieval system, or transmitted in any form or by any means, electronic, mechanical, photocopying, recording, or otherwise without either the prior written permission of the Publishers or a licence permitting restricted copying in the United Kingdom issued by the Copyright Licensing Agency Ltd, 90 Tottenham Court Road, London W1P 0LP.

First published 2000

British Library Cataloguing in Publication Data
A catalogue entry for this title is available from the British Library

ISBN 0-582-38143-6

Printed in Great Britain by Henry Ling Ltd, at the Dorset Press, Dorchester, Dorset

This is for grown-ups!

Guidance and advice

Schools are now asked to set regular homework, even for young children. Government guidelines for Year 2 (ages 6–7) suggest 1 hour of homework a week. Children are also encouraged to do at least 10–20 minutes of reading each day.

The Numeracy Hour

The daily Numeracy Hour was introduced into schools in September 1999. During this session, teachers focus on five areas: numbers and the number system; calculations; solving problems; measures, shape and space; handling data. The aim of the Numeracy Hour is to develop a child's maths skills, and give them the confidence to solve maths problems without having to ask for help.

All the activities in this book are written to complement the Numeracy Hour. The emphasis is on short, enjoyable exercises designed to stimulate a child's interest in maths. Each activity will take 10–20 minutes, depending on the topic, and the amount of drawing and colouring.

Themes and topics

Throughout the book key words have been set in **bold** text – these highlight the themes and content of the activities, and provide a guide to the topics covered.

Encourage your child

Leave your child to do the activity on their own, but be available to answer any questions. Try using phrases like: That's a good idea! How do you think you could do it? What happens if you do it this way? These will encourage your child to think about how they could answer the question for themselves.

Mental maths

Many of the activities will help children with mental maths, which is a vital part of the curriculum. Encourage your child to try to work out simple calculations in their head before writing anything down.

The activities start on the next page! Have you got your pens and pencils ready?

If your child is struggling …

Younger children might need help understanding the question before they try to work out an answer, and children who need help with reading or writing may need you to work with them. If your child is struggling with the writing, ask them to find the answer and then write it in for them. Remember even if your child gets stuck, be sure to tell them they are doing well.

Check the answers together

When they have done all they can, sit down with them and go through the answers together. Check they have not misunderstood any important part of the activity. If they have, try to show them why they are going wrong. Ask them to explain what they have done, right or wrong, so that you can understand how they are thinking.

You will find answers to the activities at the back of this book. You can remove the last page if you think your child might look at the answers before trying an activity. Sometimes there is no set answer because your child has been asked for their own ideas. Check that your child's answer is appropriate and shows they have understood the question.

Be positive!

If you think your child needs more help with a particular topic try to think of some similar but easier examples. You don't have to stick to the questions in the book – ask your own: Did you like that? Can you think of any more examples? Have a conversation about the activity. Be positive, giving praise for making an effort and understanding the question, not just getting the right answers. Your child should enjoy doing the activities and at the same time discover that learning is fun.

More on Maths

There are many activities you can do outside school that will help develop your child's familiarity with maths and provide valuable practice. Make sure your child has plenty of experience of weighing, measuring, telling the time, handling money, and sharing items out between a group. Look for opportunities to help your child practise addition, subtraction and multiplication. The more practice your child gets the more comfortable with maths they will become.

Balloons

The balloons are numbered in **tens** from 10 to 100. Some have burst.

Colour the balloons that have not burst

1. Fill in the missing numbers for the burst balloons.

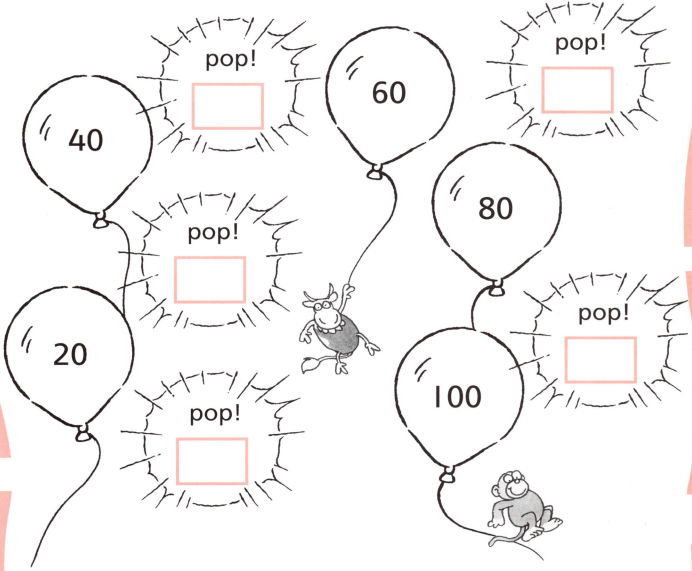

2. How many balloons have burst? _____

Domino sums

The first one has been started for you!

Fill in the boxes to complete the **number sentences** for each domino.

1

2 + 4 = ☐

2

☐ + ☐ = ☐

3

☐ + ☐ = ☐

4

☐ + ☐ = ☐

5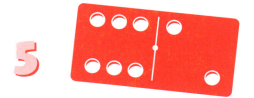

☐ + ☐ = ☐

6

☐ + ☐ = ☐

7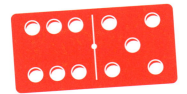

☐ + ☐ = ☐

8

☐ + ☐ = ☐

Halves

1 Count the apples.

Half of the apples are green.

Colour in the green apples.
Colour the rest of the apples red.

Half of ten apples is ...?

2 Count the flowers.

Half of the flowers are red.

Colour in the red flowers.
Colour the rest of the flowers yellow.

Count in groups

1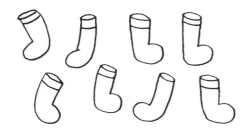

Count in twos to find out how many socks there are.

How many socks?

2

Draw rings around groups of five bees to help you count them.

How many bees?

3

Draw rings around **groups** of ten stars to help you count them.

How many stars?

Shape game

Play this fun game with a friend!
Take half of the page each.
Take turns to roll a dice.
Colour the **shape** that has the same number of sides as the number on the dice.
If there is no shape with that number of sides, colour nothing.

The winner is the first to colour all their shapes.

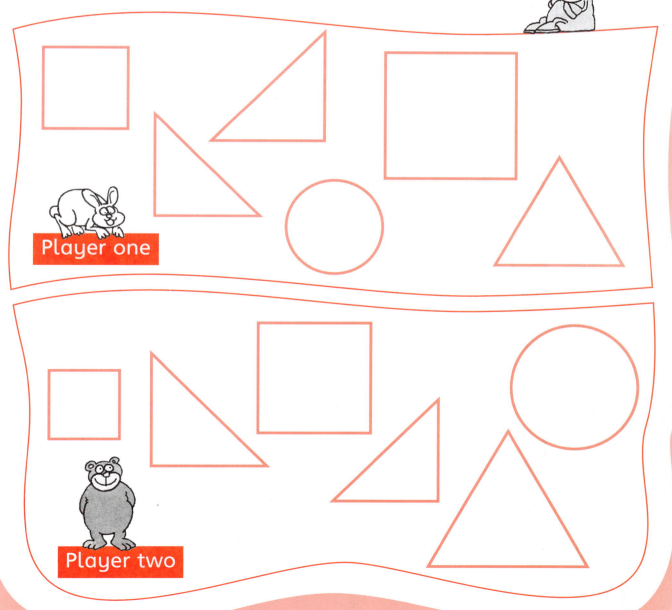

Player one

Player two

Adding to 20

Find the pairs that make **20**.

They must be next to each other

like this ⑮⑤   like this ①   or like this ⑧
                            ⑲   ⑫

Each time you find a pair of numbers that add up to 20, colour in the circles.

11	9	13	17	16
8	7	1	3	4
12	6	14	5	2
5	1	10	18	19
15	9	2	10	1

How many circles have you coloured in? _____

Hot or cold?

Here are the things Annie had for tea.

Some are hot. Some are cold.

What is your favourite cold food?

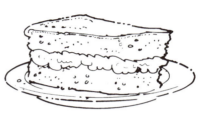

1. Lemonade and cake are _____

2. Chips, beans and burgers are _____

3. Fill in the **table**:

hot	cold
	lemonade

4. Did Annie have more hot or cold things for tea?

_____

What is your favourite hot food?

Tens and ones

You can only fit **ten** pencils into each box.

] On the chart, show how many pencils will fit into the boxes, and how many will be left out.

The first row has been filled in for you.

Total number of pencils	Number of pencils in boxes	Loose pencils	
34	30	4	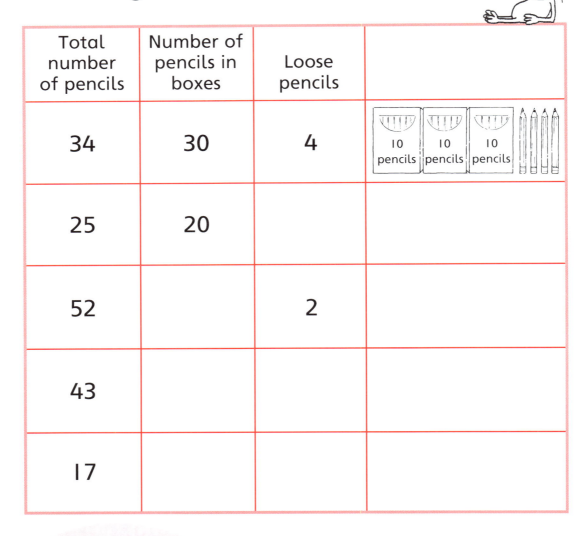
25	20		
52		2	
43			
17			

In the end column draw how many boxes and how many loose pencils.

You can use place value cards to show how two-digit numbers are made up of **tens** and **units**.

26 is made by 2 0 and 6

like this: 2 6

2 Write the numbers on the cards you would need to show these numbers.

18 → 1 0 and ☐

25 → ☐ ☐ and 5

55 → ☐ ☐ and ☐

49 → ☐ ☐ and ☐

62 → ☐ ☐ and ☐

34 → ☐ ☐ and ☐

63 → ☐ ☐ and ☐

98 → ☐ ☐ and ☐

80 → ☐ ☐ and ☐

Through the day

Look at each clock.

Write the **time** underneath it.

1

John wakes up.

_____

2

John is at school.

_____

3

John watches television.

_____

4

John goes to bed.

_____

Draw the right time on each clock.

Colour in the pictures.

At seven o'clock Mrs Patel gets up.

At half past nine she is at work.

At half past three she walks to meet her children.

At quarter to six she has tea.

More or less

 10 > 8
means 10 is
more than 8.

3 < 5
means 3 is
less than 5.

1 Put the correct sign > or < between the pairs of numbers.

58 ☐ 39   40 ☐ 28

29 ☐ 41   82 ☐ 79

57 ☐ 61   91 ☐ 92

2 Fill in the number sentences.

17 is less than 18   17 < 18

24 is less than 32

73 is more than 71

12 is more than 10

92 is less than 98

45 is more than 36

Apples

Make each pair **add up to 20** by filling in the missing numbers.

*Colour the apples with **odd** numbers blue.*

*Colour the apples with **even** numbers red.*

1
12

2
9

3
17

4
6

5
5

6
11

7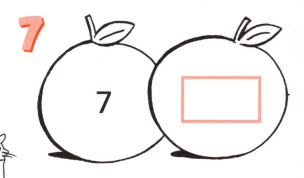
7

How many ways?

How many different ways can you go along the path?

Draw a different route in each box.

You can go **forward** → **backward** ← **down** ↓ and **up** ↑

The first one has been done for you!

Zack has gone forward, down, backward, down and forward.

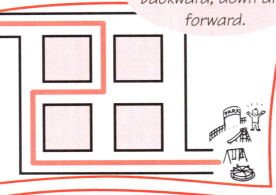
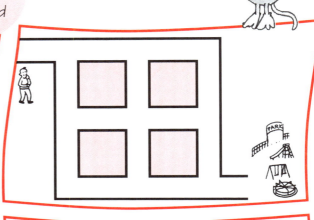
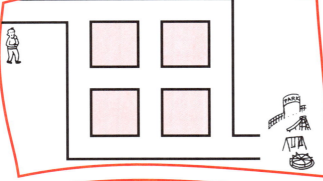
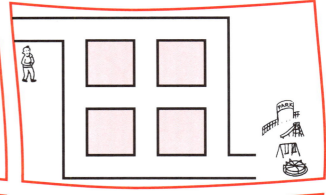

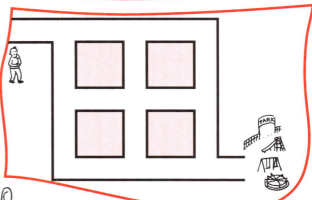

Dice game

You will need a dice and 12 counters for this.
Roll the dice.
How many more to make 10?
If the number you need is on the grid, put a counter on it.
Carry on until every number is covered.

8	4	7	8
6	5	9	5
9	7	4	6

The winner is the first to cover all their numbers.

You could play this game with a friend. Each player has half of the grid to complete.

Now try again, but this time try to make 12.

11	9	8	10
7	6	11	9
8	10	6	7

Remember, it's how many more to make 12.

How heavy?

Most bags of sugar weigh 1 kg. Find a bag. Feel how heavy it is.

Do you think these things **weigh more or less** than a bag of sugar? Tick the correct box.

1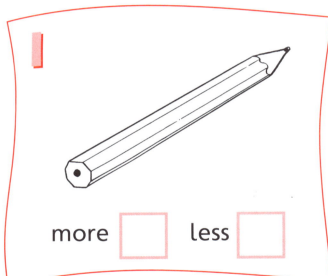

more ☐   less ☐

2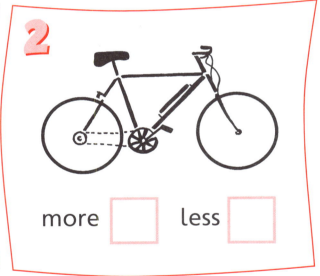

more ☐   less ☐

3

more ☐   less ☐

4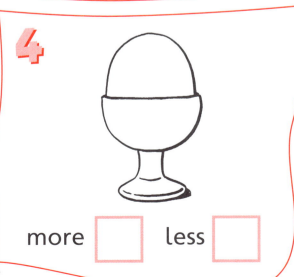

more ☐   less ☐

Sharing

Tom and Jamie had a bag of 12 lollipops.
Mum told them to take **half** each.

1 How many did Tom get? ☐

How many did Jamie get? ☐

Just then their friends Sam and Dan came to play. Mum told the boys to share the lollipops equally between them. The boys had a **quarter** of the lollipops each.

2 How many did Tom get? ☐

How many did Jamie get? ☐

How many did Sam get? ☐

How many did Dan get? ☐

3 Tom and Sam put their lollipops together in a pile.
How many were there altogether? ☐

4 Sam said, "Hey, Tom, a quarter and a quarter are the same as a _____ ."

Favourite colours

Joy asked her friends to choose their favourite colour.
She drew this **pictogram**.

number of children = 1 child

red	☺ ☺ ☺
blue	☺ ☺ ☺ ☺ ☺
yellow	☺ ☺ ☺ ☺

1 Five children liked _____

2 How many children liked yellow? _____

3 Three children liked _____

4 How many children were asked altogether? _____

5 Which was the most popular colour?

_____

3-D shapes

Draw a line to join each shape to its name.

These are 3-D shapes.

cube

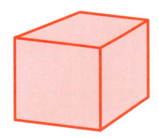

cylinder

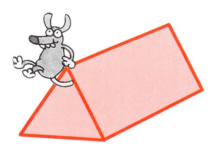

sphere

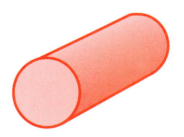

triangular prism

How many of these shapes can you find in your house?

Plain sailing

Join each boat to the right island.

The right island has the answer to the **calculation** that is on the boat.

Sweets

Each sweet has a number.

If the number is a **multiple** of 2, colour the sweet red.

If it is a **multiple** of 5, colour the sweet blue.

If the number can be divided into groups of 2, it is a multiple of 2. For instance, 6 is a multiple of 2, because it can be divided into groups of 2 like this:

If the number can be divided into groups of 5, it is a multiple of 5.

Parcel post

kg means kilograms.

Helen is sending presents to her friends.

She weighs the parcels.

Write down how much each parcel **weighs**.

1

Lee's parcel weighs

_____ kg.

2 Ali's parcel weighs

_____ kg.

3

Susie's parcel weighs

_____ kg.

4 The heaviest parcel belongs to _____ .

5 The lightest parcel belongs to _____ .

Doing and undoing

Dad gave Emma six grapes. She took three more. How many did she have?

6 + 3 = ☐

*You can "undo" an **addition** with a **subtraction**.*

Dad made her put back the three she had taken. How many were left?

9 − 3 = ☐

Use the subtracting machine to undo the addition and get back to where you started.

Adding machine	Subtracting machine
3 + 4 =	7 − = 3
5 + 6 =	− 6 = 5
8 + = 15	15 − =
+ 6 = 18	− = 12
9 + 8 =	− =
15 + = 20	− =

Flower power

Draw a line to link each flower with another. In each pair one flower must contain a number **double** the number in the other flower.

Halves and quarters

Easy adding

1 **Add** the numbers in the corners of the triangles.

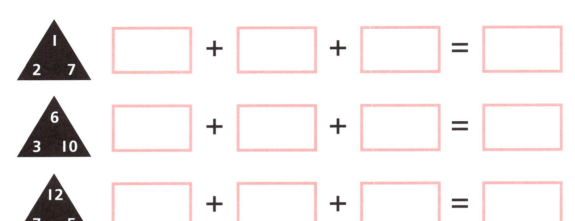

□ + □ + □ = □

□ + □ + □ = □

□ + □ + □ = □

2 Now put the largest number first and add the other numbers to it.

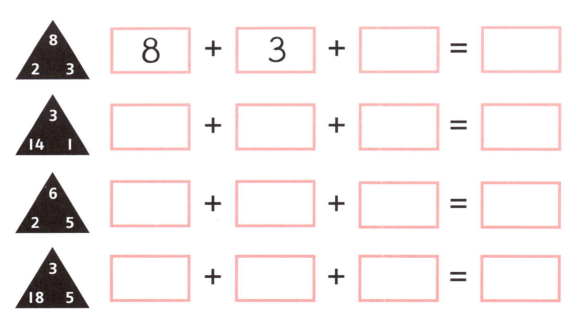

| 8 | + | 3 | + □ = □

□ + □ + □ = □

□ + □ + □ = □

□ + □ + □ = □

Did you find it easier when you put the larger number first?

3 When you add these numbers, start off by looking for pairs of numbers that make 10 or 20.

   7 + ☐ = 10, 10 + ☐ = 15

   ☐ + ☐ = 10, 10 + ☐ = ☐

   ☐ + ☐ = 10, 10 + ☐ = ☐

   ☐ + ☐ = 20, 20 + ☐ = ☐

   ☐ + ☐ = 20, 20 + ☐ = ☐

 Choose the best method for adding these numbers.

 _____

 _____

 _____

 _____

31

Number patterns

Spot the **number patterns**. Fill in the missing numbers.

Can you count in fives?

1. 5, __, 15, __, 25, __, __

2. 2, __, __, __, 10, __, 14

3. 10, __, 30, __, __, __, 70

4. 3, __, __, 12, 15, __, __

Snack time!

This **chart** shows which children ate an ice cream or an ice lolly.

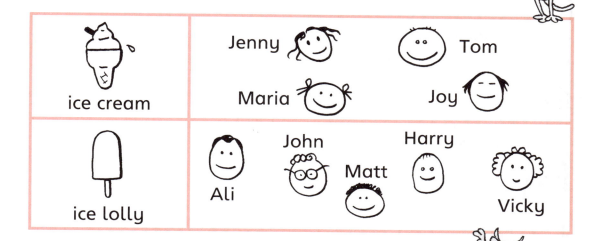

1. John ate an _____

2. Matt ate an _____

3. Maria ate an _____

4. How many children ate ice lollies? _____

5. How many ice creams were eaten? _____

6. How many girls ate ice creams? _____

7. How many boys ate ice lollies? _____

Shopping

Make sure the coins add up to the price.

Draw round the **coins** needed to buy each fruit.

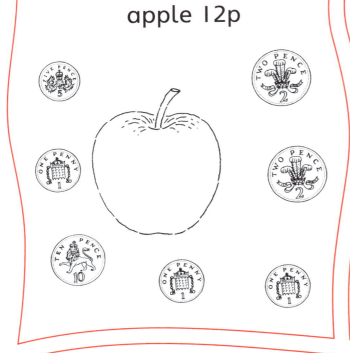

apple 12p

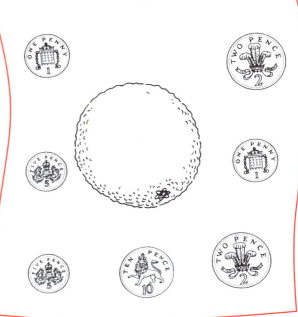

orange 15p

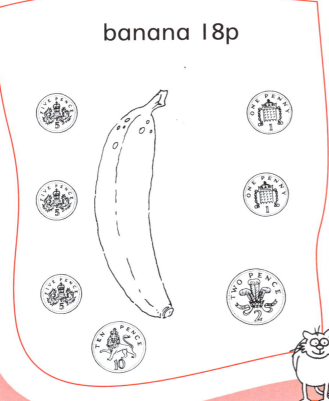

banana 18p

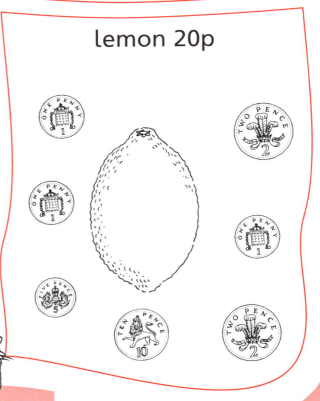

lemon 20p

How much **change** will you get?

1 ice lolly 18p

give   change

2 chocolate drops 12p

give   change

3 ice cream 15p

give   change

4 chocolate 30p

give   change

Scarves

Make each scarf different.

You will need three different coloured crayons: red, blue and yellow.

Use them to colour each scarf.

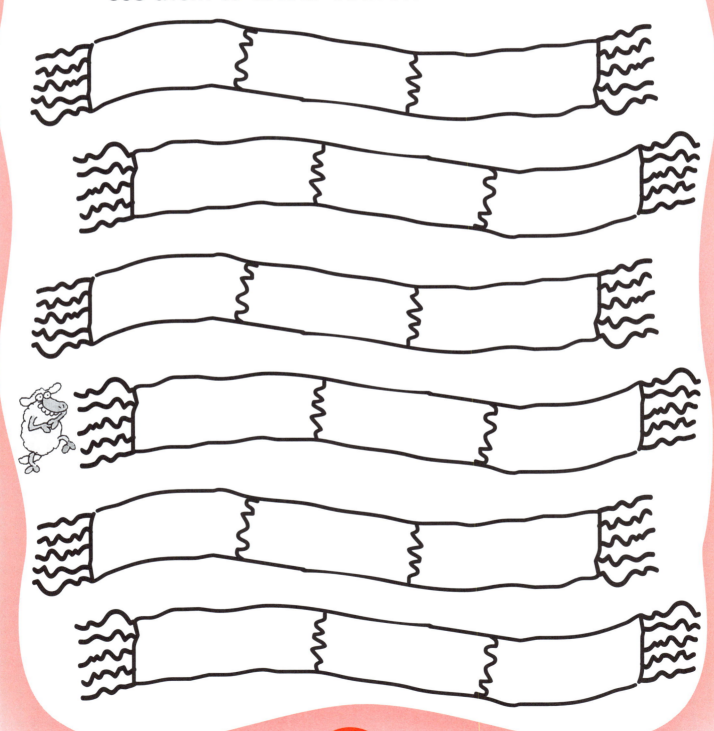

Towers

Add together two numbers that are next to each other.

Write the answer in the empty square above them.

The first one has been started for you!

Continue to do this until you reach the top of the tower.

1
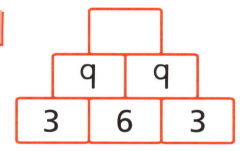

2
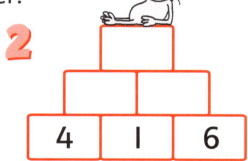

3
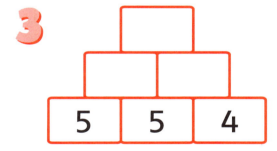

4
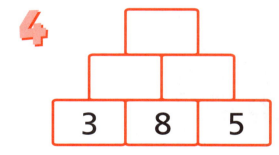

5
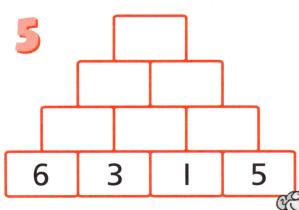

6
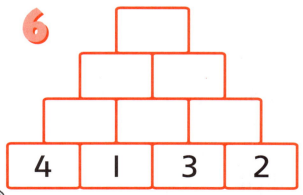

Everything in this toy shop costs **10p less** than the old label says.

Write the new prices on the empty labels.

Three in a row

Choose two numbers, one from each bin.

Add the numbers together or find the **difference** between them.

If the answer is on the grid, colour it in.

You can play this with a friend. The first to colour three squares next to each other is the winner!

Carry on until you have coloured three squares next to each other like this | 19 | 9 | 3 | or this | 7 | 3 | or this | 10 | 5 | 1 |
                                                                                                      | 8 |

1	10	19	9	3
13	2	5	13	7
9	6	9	1	8
14	1	4	12	15
2	17	3	11	14

39

Puppies

1 Give each puppy three bones.

How many bones are there altogether? ☐

2 Give each puppy five bones.

How many bones are there altogether?

3 Give each puppy two bones.

How many bones are there altogether? ☐

Drawing shapes

Draw the other half of each shape.

Make each half exactly the same.

Use the grid to help you get it right.

You will need a ruler and a sharp pencil.

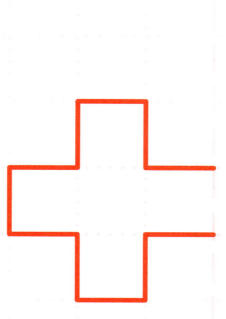

*It's like drawing a **mirror image**.*

Number lines

Fill in the missing numbers on each **number line**.

1 | 13 | 14 | | | | | | | | | 23 |

2 | 20 | | | | | | | | | | 30 |

3 | 29 | | | | | | | | | 38 | |

4 | 37 | | | 40 | | | | | | | 47 |

5 | 46 | | | | 50 | | | | 54 | | |

6 | 59 | | 61 | | | | | | | 68 |

Can you find the missing number on each line?

Which number is missing in each line?

Write it in the box.

7 22 24 ☐ 28 30 32

8 50 60 70 ☐ 90 100

9 10 15 20 25 ☐ 35

10 160 ☐ 180 190 200 210

Eye colour

This **chart** shows the eye colour of some children.

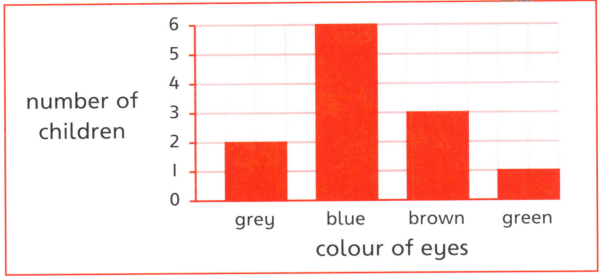

1 How many children have brown eyes? _____

2 How many children have blue eyes? _____

3 Two children have _____ eyes.

4 Only one child has _____ eyes.

5 How many more children have blue eyes than brown? _____

6 Which is the most common eye colour? _____

Hot air balloons

Find the answer to each **calculation**.

Put the answer in the box under the balloon.

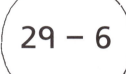
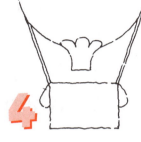

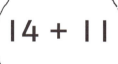
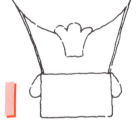
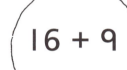

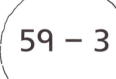

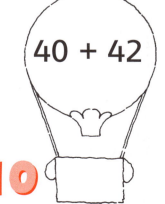

If the answer is more than 50, colour the balloon red.
If the answer is less than 50, colour the balloon blue.

In the park

Asif and Joe went to the playground in the park.

They drew a **plan** of the playground to show where things were.

To get to the swings, go along to B and then up to 3. The swings are at B3.

1 The swings are at _____

2 The climbing frame is at _____

3 The _____ is at A2.

4 The _____ is at C4.

5 Draw a roundabout at D2.

What would you put at A4? Draw it in.

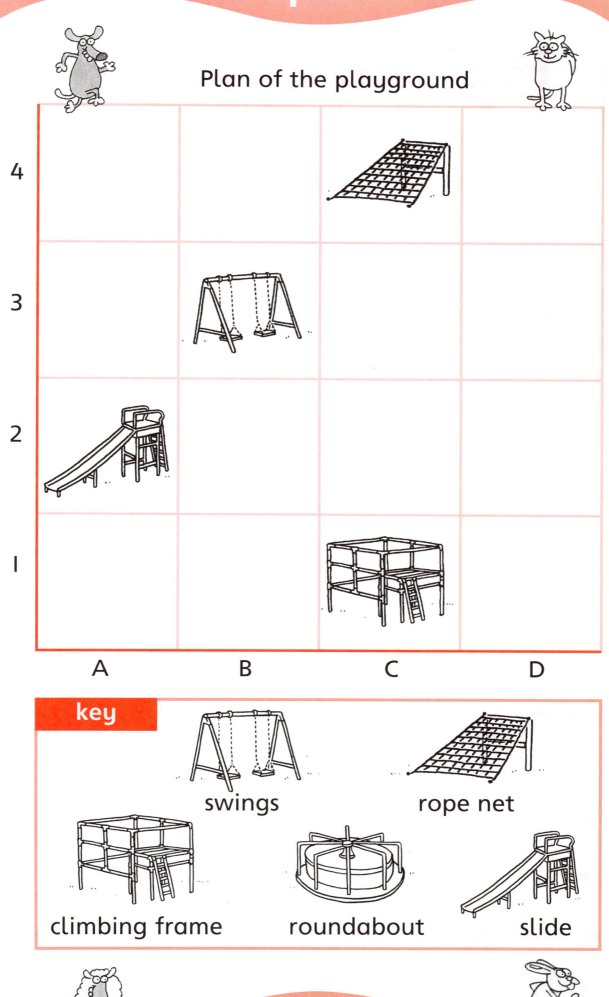

Balancing act

Each balance must have the same amount on each side.

Write the correct number in each empty box.

More **adding** practice!

The number you need has the same value as the two numbers added together.

1
2 + 1   ☐

2
☐   3 + 4

3
10 + 2   ☐

4
8 + 5   ☐

5
☐   5 + 6

6
9 + 4   ☐

Ice cream time!

1 An ice lolly costs _____

2 A choc ice costs _____

3 An ice cream costs _____

45p

55p

35p

4 Gillian has 50p.

   She buys an ice lolly. Her **change** is _____

5 Harry buys a choc ice.
   He gets 5p change.

   How much money did he pay with? _____

6 Which two things add up to exactly £1?

   _____ and _____

7 How much will two ice lollies cost? _____

49

How long?

Make an **estimate** of the length of each object. Then measure it with a ruler.

cm means centimetres.

'Make an estimate' means 'make a guess'.

1 I think the worm is ☐ cm long.

The worm measures ☐ cm.

2 I think the train is ☐ cm long.

The train measures ☐ cm.

3 I think the comb is ☐ cm long.

The comb measures ☐ cm.

4 I think the crayon is ☐ cm long.

The crayon measures ☐ cm.

5 I think the chocolate bar is ☐ cm long.

The chocolate bar measures ☐ cm.

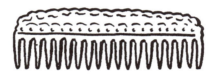

Dice fun

Roll a dice.

If the number you get completes one of these **calculations**, then write the number in. Carry on until all the calculations are completed.

1 ☐ + 2 = 3   **2** ☐ + 2 = 6

3 7 + ☐ = 11   **4** 4 + ☐ = 7

5 2 + 3 = ☐   **6** 1 + 5 = ☐

7 5 + ☐ = 7   **8** 3 + ☐ = 8

9 ☐ + 6 = 9   **10** ☐ + 9 = 10

11 4 + 2 = ☐   **12** 3 + 1 = ☐

Missing shapes

Finish drawing the **shapes**. Follow the **pattern** that has been started for you.

You must put the shapes in order so that the patten is repeated.

Colour the triangles blue,
the circles yellow,
the hexagons red,
the rectangles green.

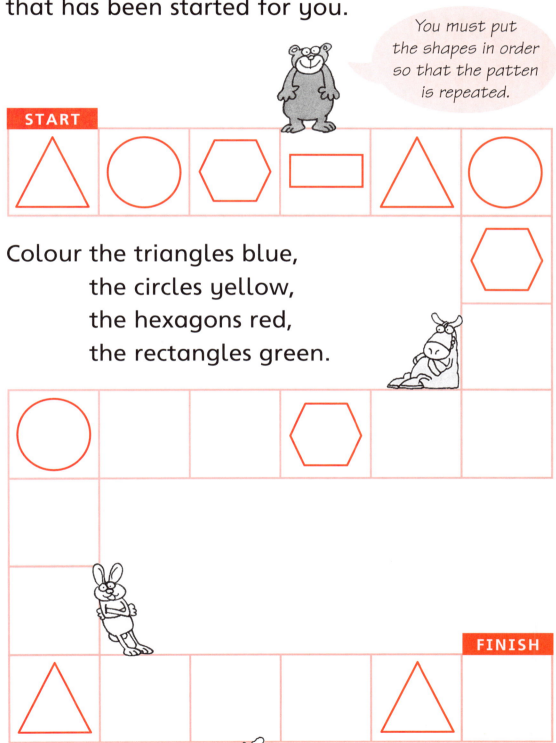

Make 100

1 Join the number pairs that make 100.

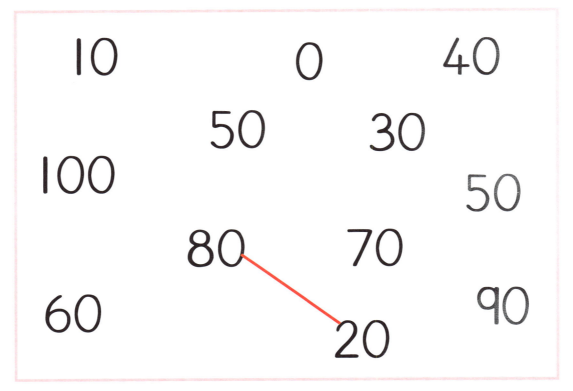

 One has been done for you.

2 Complete the number sentences.

10 + ☐ = 100   40 + ☐ = 100

70 + ☐ = 100   50 + ☐ = 100

20 + ☐ = 100   100 + ☐ = 100

Take away nine

1	2	3	4	5	6	7	8	9	10
11	12	13	14	15	16	17	18	19	20
21	22	23	24	25	26	27	28	29	30
31	32	33	34	35	36	37	38	39	40
41	42	43	44	45	46	47	48	49	50

*An easy way to **take away nine** is to take away ten and then add one on.*

1 35 − 9 = ?

Start at 35. Count back 9. You land on ☐

This is the same as:
Start at 35. Count back 10. You land on ☐

Count on 1 ☐

2 Find the answers to these sums in the same way.

27 − 9   27 − 10 = ☐ ➔ ☐ + 1 = ☐

27 − 9 = ☐

44 − 9   44 − 10 = ☐ ➔ ☐ + 1 = ☐

44 − 9 = ☐

32 − 9   32 − 10 = ☐ ➔ ☐ + 1 = ☐

32 − 9 = ☐

55

Odd or even?

Look at these numbers.

4	15	11	19	12
3	9	16		2

Sort them into two **sets**.

odd   even

Now write the numbers in the correct place in this **Carroll diagram**.

	less than 10	more than 10
odd		
even		

Brick wall

Each brick in the picture has a calculation in it. Find all the bricks which have **20** as their answer. Colour them yellow.

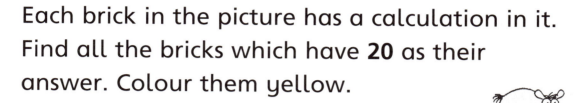

| 2 + 8 | 19 + 1 | 12 + 8 | 10 − 1 |

| 14 + 6 | 10 − 2 | 5 + 15 | 8 − 3 |

| 11 − 6 | 11 + 9 | 9 − 3 | 10 + 10 |

| 11 − 3 | 18 + 2 | 14 − 3 | 3 + 17 |

Favourite fruits

Mrs Mason asked her class to name their favourite fruit.

They drew this **bar chart**.

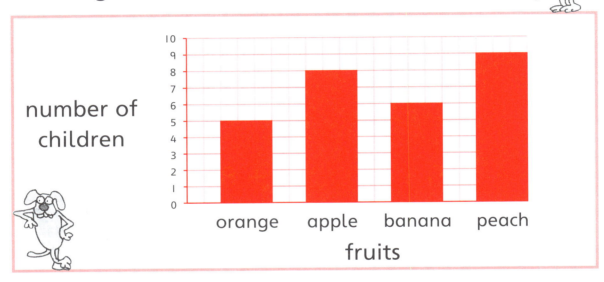

1. How many children liked apples? _____

2. Six children liked _____

3. How many children liked oranges? _____

4. Nine children liked _____

5. How many children were in the class? _____

6. What was the most popular fruit? _____

Lots and lots

These counters are laid out in a grid.

You can find out how many counters there are by **adding** or by **multiplying**.

3 + 3 + 3 = ☐

3 lots of 3 = ☐

3 × 3 = ☐

How many counters?

1

2 + 2 + 2 + 2 = ☐

4 lots of 2 = ☐

4 × 2 = ☐

2

5 + 5 = ☐

2 lots of 5 = ☐

2 × 5 = ☐

3

3 + 3 + 3 + 3 = ☐

4 lots of 3 = ☐

4 × 3 = ☐

4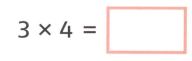

4 + 4 + 4 = ☐

3 lots of 4 = ☐

3 × 4 = ☐

Money, money

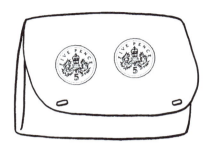

1 How much money is in this purse? ____

You spend 6p.
How much is left?

_____

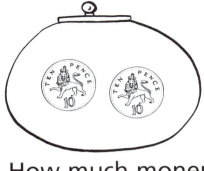

2 How much money is in this purse? ____

Half of this is

_____

3 How much money is in this purse? ____

You spend 5p.
How much is left?

_____

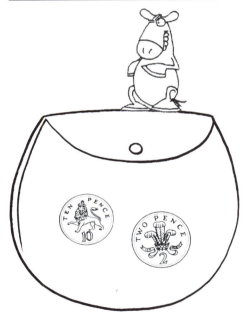

4 How much money is in this purse? ____

Half of this is

_____

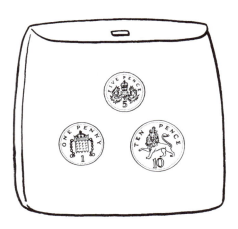

5 How much money is in this purse? ____

Double this is

_____

6 How much money is in this purse? ____

Double this is

_____

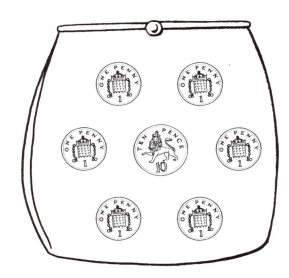
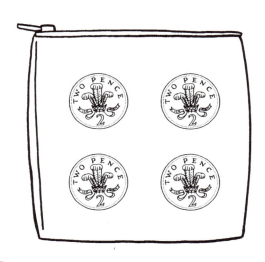

7 How much money is in this purse? ____

Add 8p.
Now there is

_____

8 How much money is in this purse? ____

Add 9p.
Now there is

_____

Targets

*This will help you practise your **tables**.*

TARGET 2

Roll two dice.
Add the numbers together.
Multiply the total by 2.
If the answer is on the target, colour the segment.
Keep going until all the segments are coloured.

Now try TARGET 10

Roll two dice.
Add the numbers together.
Multiply the total by 10.
If the answer is on the target, colour the segment.

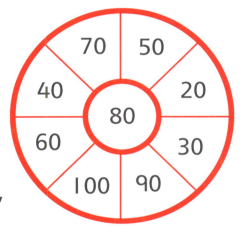

Now try TARGET 5

This is almost the same as TARGET 10, but this time, you multiply the total by 5.

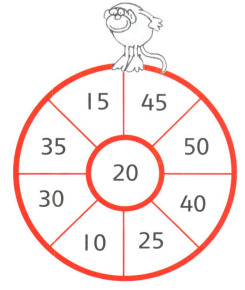

Answers and Hints

In some instances there may be more than one possible answer and you may need to check that the answer your child has given is reasonable. It is useful to go through the answers with your child to check that they have understood the question and the method of reaching the answer. Remember there may be more than one way to reach an answer.

PAGE 5
1 missing numbers: 10, 30, 50, 70, 90   **2** 5

PAGE 6
1 2 + 4 = 6   **2** 5 + 2 = 7   **3** 3 + 1 = 4   **4** 3 + 4 = 7
5 6 + 2 = 8   **6** 5 + 4 = 9   **7** 5 + 3 = 8   **8** 6 + 5 = 11

PAGE 7
Check that your child has coloured the right number of apples and flowers.   **1** 5 apples coloured green   **2** 8 flowers coloured red   Make sure they colour whole apples or flowers (but colour half the total number) rather than colouring half of every apple or flower.

PAGE 8
1 8   **2** 32   **3** 55

PAGE 9
This helps your child with recognising shapes. Make sure your child knows that a circle has only one side.

PAGE 10
Your child should have coloured ten pairs of numbers: 11 + 9, 8 + 12, 7 + 13, 17 + 3, 16 + 4, 6 + 14, 2 + 18, 5 + 15, 10 + 10, 19 + 1. A maximum of 20 circles can be coloured in altogether.

PAGE 11
1 cold   **2** hot   **3** in the table: (hot) chips, beans, burgers; (cold) lemonade, cake   **4** Annie had more hot things for tea

PAGES 12 & 13
1 25 = 2 boxes + 5 pencils, 52 = 5 boxes + 2 pencils, 43 = 4 boxes + 3 pencils, 17 = 1 box + 7 pencils
2 18 = 10, 8; 25 = 20, 5; 55 = 50, 5; 49 = 40, 9; 62 = 60, 2; 34 = 30, 4; 63 = 60, 3; 98 = 90, 8; 80 = 80, 0

PAGES 14 & 15
1 8.00 (8 o'clock)   **2** 10.15 (quarter past ten)
3 4.45 (quarter to five)   **4** 7.30 (half past seven)
5, 6, 7 & 8 check that the clocks are drawn with the correct times

PAGE 16
1 58 > 39, 40 > 28, 29 < 41, 82 > 79, 57 < 61, 91 < 92
2 24 < 32, 73 > 71, 12 > 10, 92 < 98, 45 > 36

PAGE 17
1 12 and 8   **2** 11 and 9   **3** 3 and 17   **4** 14 and 6
5 5 and 15   **6** 11 and 9   **7** 7 and 13

PAGE 18
Check that your child has chosen five different routes (there are lots of possible routes).

PAGE 19
Watch your child while they are playing to check that they are adding accurately. You could play it with them (use half the grid each).

PAGE 20
1 less   **2** more   **3** more   **4** less

PAGE 21
1 Tom and Jamie both got 6 lollipops   **2** all the boys got 3 lollipops each   **3** 6   **4** a quarter and a quarter are the same as a half

PAGE 22
1 blue   **2** 4   **3** red   **4** 12   **5** blue

PAGE 23
drawn shapes: (top to bottom) sphere, cube, triangular prism, cylinder

PAGE 24
Your child should have connected three boats to each island: 10 = 5 + 5 and 9 + 1 and 4 + 6; 15 = 13 + 2 and 9 + 6 and 5 + 10; 20 = 19 + 1 and 10 + 10 and 11 + 9.

PAGE 25
red sweets: 4, 6, 8, 12, 14, 16, 18; blue sweets: 5, 15, 25, 35, 45

PAGE 26
1 2   **2** 3   **3** 1   **4** Ali   **5** Susie

PAGE 27
6 + 3 = 9, 9 − 3 = 6   adding machine: 3 + 4 = 7, 7 − 4 = 3; 5 + 6 = 11, 11 − 6 = 5; 8 + 7 = 15, 15 − 7 = 8 or 15 − 8 = 7; 12 + 6 = 18, 18 − 6 = 12; 9 + 8 = 17 subtracting machine: 17 − 8 = 9 or 17 − 9 = 8; 15 + 5 = 20, 20 − 5 = 15 or 20 − 15 = 5

PAGE 28
pairs of flowers: 5 and 10, 6 and 12, 7 and 14, 8 and 16, 9 and 18

PAGE 29
Check that your child has coloured the correct portion of each shape (either a half or a quarter).

PAGES 30 & 31
1 2 + 1 + 7 = 10, 3 + 6 + 10 = 19, 7 + 12 + 5 = 24
2 8 + 3 + 2 = 13, 14 + 3 + 1 = 18, 6 + 5 + 2 = 13, 18 + 3 + 5 = 26   **3** 7 + 3 = 10, 10 + 5 = 15; 8 + 2 = 10, 10 + 9 = 19; 4 + 6 = 10, 10 + 5 = 15; 13 + 7 = 20, 20 + 8 = 28; 5 + 15 = 20, 20 + 2 = 22   The best methods for adding these numbers are probably: 7 + 2 + 5 = 14; 9 + 1 = 10, 10 + 3 = 13; 13 + 2 = 15, 15 + 5 = 20; 18 + 2 = 20, 20 + 4 = 24.

PAGE 32
1 (missing numbers) 10, 20, 30, 35   **2** 4, 6, 8, 12   **3** 20, 40, 50, 60   **4** 6, 9, 18, 21

PAGE 33
1 ice lolly   **2** ice lolly   **3** ice cream   **4** 5   **5** 4   **6** 3
7 4

PAGES 34 & 35
There are various ways of circling the money in each case; check your child has chosen coins that add up to make the correct amount **1** 2p **2** 8p **3** 5p **4** 20p

PAGE 36
Check that all the scarves are coloured differently. If your child used all three colours on each scarf there are six possible patterns. If instead they used only one or two colours on each scarf there are a further 21 different patterns (27 in all). Encourage your child to draw out more scarves and colour them in; investigation activities encourage your child to solve problems in a logical way. Children are often surprised at the number of different ways it is possible to colour the scarves using just three colours.

PAGE 37
1 (top) 18 **2** (top) 12; (second row) 5, 7 **3** (top) 19; (second row) 10, 9 **4** (top) 24; (second row) 11, 13
5 (top) 23; (second row) 13, 10; (third row) 9, 4, 6
6 (top) 18; (second row) 9, 9; (third row) 5, 4, 5

PAGE 38
new prices: (top shelf) 80p, 40p; (bottom shelf) 24p, 55p

PAGE 39
This game helps your child practise addition and subtaction. If your child wanted to play the game again, they could use counters to cover the numbers, or draw out their own grid.

PAGE 40
1 6 **2** 10 **3** 6

PAGE 41
Check that your child has drawn a correct mirror image for each shape.

PAGES 42 & 43
1 (missing numbers) 15, 16, 17, 18, 19, 20, 21, 22
2 21, 22, 23, 24, 25, 26, 27, 28, 29 **3** 30, 31, 32, 33, 34, 35, 36, 37, 39 **4** 38, 39, 41, 42, 43, 44, 45, 46
5 47, 48, 49, 51, 52, 53, 55, 56 **6** 60, 62, 63, 64, 65, 66, 67, 69 **7** 26 **8** 80 **9** 30 **10** 170 For more practice at this, you could cover one number at a time with a small piece of paper and ask your child to name the missing number.

PAGE 44
1 3 **2** 6 **3** grey **4** green **5** 3 **6** blue

PAGE 45
1 59 **2** 34 **3** 23 **4** 52 **5** 25 **6** 27 **7** 25 **8** 56
9 19 **10** 82 Check that your child has coloured balloons 1, 4, 8 & 10 red

PAGES 46 & 47
1 B3 **2** C1 **3** slide **4** rope ladder **5** check that your child has drawn the roundabout at D2

PAGE 48
1 3 **2** 7 **3** 12 **4** 13 **5** 11 **6** 13

PAGE 49
1 35p **2** 45p **3** 55p **4** 15p **5** 50p **6** choc ice and ice cream **7** 70p

PAGES 50 & 51
1 (actual length) 12 cm **2** 8 cm **3** 5 cm **4** 4 cm
5 10 cm

PAGE 52
Check that for any throw of the dice your child writes in the correct answer and their calculations are accurate. **1** 1 **2** 4 **3** 4 **4** 3 **5** 5 **6** 6 **7** 2 **8** 5
9 3 **10** 1 **11** 6 **12** 4

PAGE 53
Check that your child has completed the sentence and coloured the shapes correctly: blue triangle, yellow circle, red hexagon, green rectangle.

PAGE 54
1 0 and 100, 10 and 90, 30 and 70, 40 and 60, 50 and 50 **2** missing numbers: (left column, top to bottom) 90, 30, 80; (right column) 60, 50, 0

PAGE 55
1 26, 25, 26 **2** 27 − 10 = 17, 17 + 1 = 18, 27 − 9 = 18; 44 − 10 = 34, 34 + 1 = 35, 44 −9 = 35; 32 − 10 = 22, 22 + 1 = 23, 32 − 9 = 23

PAGE 56
odd numbers: (less than 10) 3, 9; (more than 10) 11, 15, 19; even numbers : (less than 10) 2, 4; (more than 10) 12, 16

PAGE 57
Your child should have coloured 8 bricks yellow (18 + 2, 3 + 17, 11 + 9, 10 + 10, 14 + 6, 5 + 15, 19 + 1, 12 + 8)

PAGE 58
1 8 **2** banana **3** 5 **4** peach **5** 28 **6** peach

PAGE 59
Check that your child understands that '3 + 3 + 3', '3 lots of 3' and '3 × 3' all represent the same sum and all equal 9. **1** they all equal 8 **2** they all equal 10
3 they all equal 12 **4** they all equal 12

PAGES 60 & 61
1 10p, 4p **2** 20p, 10p **3** 12p, 7p **4** 12p, 6p **5** 16p, 32p **6** 9p, 18p **7** 16p, 24p **8** 8p, 17p

PAGE 62
This game provides a good opportunity for your child to practise their 2, 5 and 10 times tables. You can play the game with them. If your child wanted to play again, they could use small counters to cover the numbers, or draw out their own targets.